W9-BWT-428

Stark County District Library
www.StarkLibrary.org
330.452.0665

MAR   2019

DISCARDED

TURTLES

Darla Duhaime

Rourke
Educational Media

rourkeeducationalmedia.com

Scan for Related Titles
and Teacher Resources

Before & After Reading Activities

Teaching Focus

Reading Comprehension- Use specific comprehension strategies, such as the use of story structure, to help students increase their reading comprehension.

Before Reading:

Building Academic Vocabulary and Background Knowledge

Before reading a book, it is important to set the stage for your child or student by using pre-reading strategies. This will help them develop their vocabulary, increase their reading comprehension, and make connections across the curriculum.

1. *Read the title and look at the cover. Let's make predictions about what this book will be about.*
2. *Take a picture walk by talking about the pictures/photographs in the book. Implant the vocabulary as you take the picture walk. Be sure to talk about the text features such as headings, Table of Contents, glossary, bolded words, captions, charts/diagrams, or Index.*
3. Have students read the first page of text with you then have students read the remaining text.
4. *Strategy Talk – use to assist students while reading.*
    - *Get your mouth ready*
    - *Look at the picture*
    - *Think…does it make sense*
    - *Think…does it look right*
    - *Think…does it sound right*
    - *Chunk it – by looking for a part you know*
5. *Read it again.*

Content Area Vocabulary
Use glossary words in a sentence.

environment
hatch
lungs
warmth

After Reading:

Comprehension and Extension Activity

After reading the book, work on the following questions with your child or students in order to check their level of reading comprehension and content mastery.

1. *What are three things all reptiles have in common?* (Summarize)
2. *Does having lungs make you a reptile?* (Asking Questions)
3. *Name two things that make you different from reptiles.* (Text to self connection)
4. *Why can't turtles stay underwater all the time?* (Asking Questions)

Extension Activity

Make your own turtle shell! Draw a large circle on a piece of poster board. Make sure it is large enough to cover your back. With the help of an adult, cut out the circle and decorate it. Make two tiny holes on each side, about six inches apart. Thread a piece of yarn through the holes and secure. Make sure you use enough yarn for your arms to fit into the loops you create. Your shell is ready to wear!

Table of Contents

Turtles are Reptiles

Reptiles are cold blooded. A reptile's body cannot make its own **warmth.**

Turtles are reptiles. Are they cold blooded?

Turtles need heat from the **environment** to make their bodies warm.

skin

Reptiles have dry, scaly skin. What kind of skin does a turtle have?

Baby Turtles

Most reptiles lay eggs. Does a turtle lay eggs?

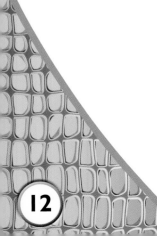

eggs

nest

Turtles spend a lot of time in the water. They make nests on land to lay their eggs.

Dig, dig! After they **hatch**, it can take baby turtles a few days to dig out of the nest.

Reptiles have **lungs**. They need air to breathe. Do turtles need air?

Turtles can stay underwater for hours.
But they must come up to breathe.

You must come up for air when you swim, too. Are YOU a reptile?

Picture Glossary

 **environment** (en-VYE-ruhn-muhnt): The natural surroundings of living things, such as the air, land, or sea.

 **hatch** (hatch): When an egg hatches, it breaks open and a baby reptile or bird comes out.

 **lungs** (luhngs): A pair of baglike organs that fill with air when an animal or person breathes.

 **warmth** (wormth): The sensation of being warm.

Index

Websites to Visit

http://easyscienceforkids.com/tag/all-about-turtles-for-kids

https://kidskonnect.com/animals/turtle

http://discoverykids.com/articles/all-about-turtles-and-tortoises

About the Author

Darla Duhaime is fascinated by all the cool things animals and people can do. When she's not writing books for kids, she enjoys eating strange foods, daydreaming, and cloud-watching. She likes to stay active and is known for keeping things interesting at family gatherings.

Meet The Author!
www.meetREMauthors.com

© 2017 Rourke Educational Media

All rights reserved. No part of this book may be reproduced or utilized in any form or by any means, electronic or mechanical including photocopying, recording, or by any information storage and retrieval system without permission in writing from the publisher.

www.rourkeeducationalmedia.com

PHOTO CREDITS: Cover © Ryan M. Bolton-Shutterstock; title page © Jamie Farrant; page 5 © bardelweb; page 6 © PAKULA PIOTR; page 8 © nutaomnice; page 10 © eve_eve01genesis; page 13 © german; page 14 © davidevison; page 16 © Karla Martinez; page 18 © Eric Isselee; page 20 © Andrey Danilovich; page 22 © Tom Wang

Edited by: Keli Sipperley
Cover design by: Nicola Stratford - www.nicolastratford.com
Interior design by: Jen Thomas

Library of Congress PCN Data

Turtles/ Darla Duhaime
(Reptiles)
ISBN (hard cover)(alk. paper) 978-1-68342-157-3
ISBN (soft cover) 978-1-68342-199-3
ISBN (e-Book) 978-1-68342-227-3
Library of Congress Control Number: 2016956589

Printed in the United States of America, North Mankato, Minnesota

Also Available as:

ROURKE'S
e-Books

3 1333 04778 4135